# Faith Over Fear

**TRACI JACO**

# FAITH *over* FEAR

LEARNING TO WALK BY
FAITH EVERYDAY

**TRACI JACO**

© 2019 by Traci Jaco

All rights reserved. This book or any portion thereof may not be reproduced or used in any manner whatsoever without the express written permission of the publisher except for the use of brief quotations in a book review.

ISBN: 9781090322005

This book is lovingly dedicated to my wonderful family. To my husband, Jeff, I'm thankful for your constant love and support for more than twenty-three years. You still make my heart skip a beat. To my two miracles, Jay and Hope, I'm thankful that doctors are not always right. I am so thankful to God for you and thrilled to be your momma.

This book is also dedicated in loving memory to Robert Remington Stockdale, February 7, 2019
Your short presence in our lives taught us much about faith and changed our lives forever.

# Contents

Forward                                           11

1. Exposing the Motive of the Enemy               13

2. Is Faith Really Connected to Righeousness?     21

3. Seeking & Rewarding                            29

4. Is Fear Taught?                                39

5. A Decision to be Made                          47

6. Faith with Legs                                55

7. How Important is it Anyway?                    65

# Forward

He called me when I was a young girl. I'm not sure why other than the fact that my parents made Him our family's priority, so He became my priority too. I remember wanting to please Him. I had no doubt that He loved me. I ate up every lesson from my Sunday school teachers and every song sung in worship. So many of my childhood memories are centered around church. Did I get somewhat wayward as a teenager? Of course. Didn't you? But no matter how much the world pulled at me, His love and grace pulled more. Forgiveness that flowed so freely made me love Him more.

Still, I had an enemy. The enemy knew that it was unlikely that he would defeat me with the temptation of blatant sin, although it did at times have its pull. No, he would have to be a little more subtle than that. How about fear?

Fear. It was generational in my family. So, alongside faith, I learned fear. Who taught me fear? That's not important. What is important is that even generational sin and curses can and must be broken. (We will talk more about this at a later time.)

The enemy knew that without faith I couldn't even please God. If he could just get my focus on fear, then he could get my faith to shake, and ultimately my righteousness would be unrighteousness.

It was a perfect plan and would have worked, except for the fact that I learned some lessons from King David and asked God to reveal the plan of my enemy to me…and He did.

As we begin this journey of revelation and victory, I want to put a thought into your mind that hopefully, by the end of this book, will make its way into your heart.

"It is not that fear is never present, it's that my faith is more present."

—*Traci Jaco, March 2019*

# 1

## EXPOSING THE MOTIVE OF THE ENEMY

What is it that is keeping you from living in absolute victory? For many who have picked up this book, it is fear. The truth is that most of us have more than one thing that is keeping us feeling defeated. What is it? Your past, addiction, harmful relationships? The list could go on. One of the most challenging verses (for me) is Psalm 15:1–2,

> *A Psalm of David. "LORD, who may abide in Your tabernacle? Who may dwell in Your holy hill? He who walks uprightly, works righteousness, and speaks the truth in his heart..."*

Are you speaking the truth in your heart? It is so easy for us to deceive ourselves. Our goal is to identify what our greatest struggle is. Can you take some time today to sincerely ask God to show you what is keeping you from victory? Are you willing to see the truth that is in your heart? If the answer comes easily for you, the next step is to ask God to show you how to overcome what you are struggling with.

For example: "Father, I know that my battle is with fear. Please show me how to defeat my enemy and have victory in every area of my life!" If you are willing, He will open your eyes.

**OUR GOAL IS TO IDENTIFY WHAT OUR GREATEST STRUGGLE IS.**

For me, the struggle was fear and anxiety. (To learn more about my testimony, I would love for you to read my devotional *What Shall I Fear?*) I began to ask God to show me how to defeat the fear and anxiety that was totally taking over my life. And guess what? He did!

One morning as I was reading my Bible, God absolutely revealed to me the motive of my enemy, and it made me shake myself out of the fog of fear that had engulfed me and gave me my fight back. This is the verse that changed my path:

> *"By faith Abel offered to God a more excellent sacrifice than Cain, through which he obtained witness that he was righteous, God testifying of his gifts; and through it he being dead still speaks." (Heb. 11:4).*

My friend, when I read, "through which he obtained witness that he was righteous," I almost fell over. Abel's sacrifice that he offered by *faith* was a witness of his *righteousness*. Righteous: (*dik'-ah-yos*) "By implication innocent, holy (absolutely or relatively): just, meet, right (-eous)" (Strong's Hebrew and Greek Dictionary).

Praise God that His righteousness is applied to our lives! He makes us "innocent and holy." But as I read this scripture, a thought came to my mind: If Abel's faith was a testimony of his righteousness, what is my fear testifying about me? What will the testimony of my life be? "Traci Jaco had great fear?" No! I want the testimony of my life to say, "Traci Jaco knew her God and was a woman of faith!"

Then I understood. The enemy was not attacking me with fear just to torment me. He hates my soul. He hates my relationship with God. He also knows the Word of God and knows that if I don't have faith, *I can't even please God.*

> *"But without faith it is impossible to please Him…" (Heb. 11:6).*

When I understood that the enemy was using the tool of fear to get between me and the Lover of My Soul, it was as if pure steel had been poured into my spirit and my backbone. You see, I have put too much into this relationship with God to allow the enemy to get me distracted with fear. My strength rose up in me and said, "Oh no you don't! I love Him. You *will not* come between me and my God."

This is how it works: you are in love with Jesus. Your eyes are fully focused on Him. You trust Him. You know how awesome and powerful He is and that He loves you. Then one day because of a thought, crazy hormones, horrible news from afar, or an unexpected diagnosis, fear enters your mind and heart. The next thing you know, your eyes have shifted from The All Powerful One to fear, and your emotions back up every horrible thing that enters your mind. Fear and anxiety say, "You better not trust Him. Keep on your guard. Keep looking at me." Fear makes you question God.

And you ask: "Where is He?" My dear friend, He is still there and still in love with you and still as powerful as He has ever been. Fear has just taken your eyes off of Him.

Let's get our eyes back on Jesus and teach our faith to soar!

*Notes*

*Notes*

# 2

## IS FAITH REALLY CONNECTED TO RIGHEOUSNESS?

I can only imagine what you are thinking: "OK, so this may have been a revelation to you, and I can see the connection between Abel's faith and his righteousness, but I need more proof to believe that all this 'mess' of fear that I have gone through is the enemy trying to disrupt my relationship with God."

I'm so glad you asked! Let's take a closer look at the connection between faith and righteousness.

What is Hebrews 11? It's the "Hall of Faith," story after story about people faced with situations that required such faith in God! In verse 7 the connection between faith and righteousness is clearly laid out: *"But without faith it is impossible to please Him..." (Heb. 11:6).* Just to please Him, we must have faith. Isn't this what we all want? *I want to please him!*

This "please" in Hebrews 6 is from the Greek word *euaresteō (yoo-ar-es-teh'-o),* which means "to *gratify entirely:* to please (well)." (Strong's Hebrew and Greek Dictionary) It brings pleasure to God when we have faith in Him!

Another confirmation we have in scripture that faith is connected to righteousness is in the very next verse. "By faith Noah, being divinely warned of things not yet seen, moved with godly fear, prepared an ark for the saving of his household, by which he condemned the world *and became heir of the righteousness which is according to faith*" (Heb. 11:7).

Noah became "heir of the righteousness which is *according* to faith." There is a righteousness that is in direct correlation to your faith. I don't know what that does in your heart, but it makes me want to shout to the world that I have faith in God.

We also see an example of this in James, chapter 2, which speaks of Abraham. *"Was not Abraham our father justified by works when he offered Isaac his son on the altar?" (James 2:22).* Do you see that faith was working together with his works, and by works faith was made perfect?

And the Scripture was fulfilled that says, *"Abraham believed God, and it was accounted to Him for righteousness* (James 2:23). And he was called the friend of God.

Abraham's faith in God was accounted as righteousness! My dear friend, your enemy and mine is after our righteousness. Why do you think that our having faith in God can please Him or make Him look at us as righteous?

For those of you who have children, nieces, nephews, or grandchildren, how does it make you feel when they don't trust you? My daughter has dealt with a lot of fear (unfortunately, taught by me.) If she is about to do something that she sees as fearful or dangerous, and I assure her that I will be right with her, and she will be fine, she will REPEATEDLY ask me, "You will be right with me, right?" I could tell her a hundred times, but she will ask again. It frustrates me until I say, "Hope, I told you that I will not leave you. Why don't you trust me?"

I can only image that God would feel the same frustration when the people that He has shed his blood for look at Him with questioning eyes that say, "Are You sure You are in control, and I can trust You?"

We see an example of this in Isaiah, chapter 30 when the children of Israel were going to Egypt for help instead of turning to God.

> *"Woe to the rebellious children," says the LORD,*
> *"Who take counsel, but not of Me,*
> *And who devise plans, but not of My Spirit,*
> *That they may add sin to sin;*
> *Who walk to go down to Egypt,*
> *And have not asked My advice,*

*Is Faith Really Connected to Righteous?*

> *To strengthen themselves in the strength of Pharaoh,*
> *And to trust in the shadow of Egypt!*
> *Therefore the strength of Pharaoh*
> *Shall be your shame,*
> *And trust in the shadow of Egypt*
> *Shall be your humiliation"* (Isa. 30:1–3)

These were His children and they were turning back to Egypt (the place that He had delivered them from) for help. He called this not trusting or asking for His help—sin.

The spirit of fear is a liar. It gives us a false sense of being in control. It convinces us that we must be on our guard all the time. There is never a chance to relax. We alone are responsible for making sure that our children and the people around us that we care about are safe *all of the time*. We even congratulate ourselves on being such good parents and friends. My friend, *none* of us have that much control. You are never really in control. It is false control. This hyper protectiveness makes us take our eyes off of the *truth* of God's word.

We become more confident in what fear says to us than what the Word of God says to us. It can go so far as to make us cynical in our view of God and His ability to help, protect, guide, and heal.

**WE BECOME MORE CONFIDENT IN WHAT FEAR SAYS TO US THAN WHAT THE WORD OF GOD SAYS TO US.**

Is this happening in your walk with God? Do the fears that you are facing make you want to trust in the false control of fear rather than put all your faith and confidence in God? You are His child. You bring Him great pleasure when you put your trust and confidence in Him and His Word.

Now in contrast to the children of Israel in Isaiah, let's look at a woman in Matthew 15 who had her worst fears realized. You see her daughter was "grievously vexed with a devil" and she asked Jesus to heal her. Jesus ignored her. What did she do next? She worshipped Him. Look at His response the second time:

> *But He answered and said, "It is not good to take the children's bread and throw it to the little dogs." And she said, "Yes, Lord, yet even the little dogs eat the crumbs which fall from their masters' table." Then Jesus answered and said to her, "O woman, great is your faith! Let it be to you as you desire." And her daughter was healed from that very hour (Matt. 15:26–28).*

Was Jesus trying to be mean? Of course not. That is not His nature, but let me ask you this: How do you respond when God doesn't answer your prayer the first time you ask? Are you willing to continue to worship? This woman had *no doubt* that He was able to heal her daughter, and she was willing to continue to ask and worship even when it seemed in vain. *Her faith took the form of action when she persisted in letting Him know that He could heal her daughter, and she worshipped Him for it in advance.* Her faith was rewarded. I can only imagine that there was a smile on His face and excitement in His voice when He said "O woman, great is your faith!" It pleased Him.

I have been both a person of Israel, turning to Egypt (in fear) and the woman of great faith. I have no stones to throw at you. Only you and God know which of these people you are right now.

"Noah was an heir of the righteousness that is according to faith…"

*Notes*

*Notes*

# 3
## SEEKING & REWARDING

Let's take another look at Hebrews 11:6.

*"But without faith it is impossible to please Him, for he who comes to God must believe that He is, and that He is a rewarder of those who diligently seek Him._*

First, you must believe that He is! This is the most basic part of faith, believing in the existence of God. That is probably not where most of us have our struggle. If we are honest with ourselves, we know that our struggle comes with the idea of God being a rewarder.

It's the enemy's job to make us feel alone, unwanted, and unworthy. He can easily accomplish this through fear. How? Because our fears are, more times than not, tied to our emotions.

If through our emotions the enemy can get us to question God and His word, his battle is half won. If we can just let our faith (even as a grain of a mustard seed) rise up enough to say, "I believe Your Word. I am seeking You, and You will reward my efforts," I assure you that God will take notice! You will receive the "rewards" of our King.

Let's take a look at some scriptures about *seeking*.

*"When You said, 'Seek My face,' My heart said to You, 'Your face, LORD, I will seek'" (Psalm 27:8).*

*"The young lions lack and suffer hunger; But those who seek the*

LORD shall not lack any good thing" (Psalm 34:10).

"But from there you will seek the LORD your God, and you will find Him if you seek Him with all your heart and with all your soul" (Deut. 4:29).

> Glory in His holy name;
> Let the hearts of those rejoice who seek the LORD!
> Seek the LORD and His strength;
> Seek His face evermore!
> Remember His marvelous works which He has done,
> His wonders, and the judgments of His mouth (Psalm 105:3–5).

I love this! Seek, remember, and rejoice! Take a moment right now and remember the great things that He has done for you! Seek Him and rejoice that He is the same God now as he was then. So many times, in scripture, we are admonished to remember or recall what God has done. Why is this? Because it is a testimony, and it increases our faith.

**SEEK, REMEMBER, AND REJOICE!**

To take this a step forward, Revelation 12:11 says, *"And they overcame him by the blood of the Lamb and by the word of their testimony..."*

Here are a few more:
> And those who know Your name will put their trust in You; For You, LORD, have not forsaken those who seek You.
> Sing praises to the LORD, who dwells in Zion! Declare His deeds among the people.
> When He avenges blood, He remembers them; He does not forget

*Seeking & Rewarding*

> *the cry of the humble (Psalm 9:10–12).*

> *"The poor shall eat and be satisfied; Those who seek Him will praise the LORD. Let your heart live forever!" (Psalm 22:26).*

Why am I giving you so many scriptures about God being faithful in listening to and responding to those who seek Him? Because it has been my experience that fear made me shy away from His presence. Actually being still and quiet enough to "seek Him" was a frightening thing because of the voice of fear that would be right there ready to scream at me when things were quiet. So instead of seeking Him, we seek others.

Don't get me wrong, you *need* friends that have a walk with God who will help you during an attack of fear or anxiety, but my friend, we must learn to seek Him for ourselves as well. If you are like me, and the quiet was overwhelming, then I encourage you to get this list of scriptures and shout them out to God in a loud voice! (There are also many scriptures about crying out in a loud voice to God.) Look at how many promises are given to those who seek Him. He cannot lie. If He says that He will reward your seeking, He will.

Fear makes us think that He isn't faithful, loving, a provider, healer, keeper, or defender. Some even have a fear that they are not worthy of being rewarded by God. When you are overcome with anxiety He doesn't look like a "Rewarder," but it does not matter what things look like or what God looks like in your present situation. Faith does not look at what we see right now. Faith looks ahead. Faith knows that His Word is true regardless of how things look or feel.

Moses was able to follow in faith because He understood that God was a rewarder!

> *By faith Moses, when he became of age, refused to be called the*

*son of Pharaoh's daughter, choosing rather to suffer affliction with the people of God than to enjoy the passing pleasures of sin, esteeming the reproach of Christ greater riches than the treasures in Egypt; for he looked to the reward. By faith he forsook Egypt, not fearing the wrath of the king; for he endured as seeing Him who is invisible (Heb. 11:24–27).*

Maybe your question is "How do I seek Him?" You seek Him through prayer. You do not have to be a theologian or an expert in the areas of prayer to get His attention. Just talk to Him. Tell Him everything that is in your heart. You can seek Him through His Word. Go to the Psalms and read how David and the other psalmists poured out their hearts to God. (Psalms 61, 5, and 142 are all good places to start.)

Soon, you will say with the Psalmist in Psalm 116:

1   *I love the LORD, because He has heard*
    *My voice and my supplications.*
2   *Because He has inclined His ear to me,*
    *Therefore I will call upon Him as long as I live.*
3   *The pains of death surrounded me,*
    *And the pangs of Sheol laid hold of me;*
    *I found trouble and sorrow.*
4   *Then I called upon the name of the LORD:*
    *"O LORD, I implore You, deliver my soul!"*
5   *Gracious is the LORD, and righteous;*
    *Yes, our God is merciful.*
6   *The LORD preserves the simple;*
    *I was brought low, and He saved me.*

7   Return to your rest, O my soul,
    For the LORD has dealt bountifully with you.
8   For You have delivered my soul from death,
    My eyes from tears, And my feet from falling.
9   I will walk before the LORD
    In the land of the living.
10  I believed, therefore I spoke,
    "I am greatly afflicted."
11  I said in my haste, "All men are liars."
12  What shall I render to the LORD
    For all His benefits toward me?
13  I will take up the cup of salvation,
    And call upon the name of the LORD.
14  I will pay my vows to the LORD
    Now in the presence of all His people.
15  Precious in the sight of the LORD Is the death of His saints.
16  O LORD, truly I am Your servant;
    I am Your servant, the son of Your maidservant;
    You have loosed my bonds.
17  I will offer to You the sacrifice of thanksgiving,
    And will call upon the name of the LORD.
18  I will pay my vows to the LORD
    Now in the presence of all His people,
19  In the courts of the LORD's house,
    In the midst of you, O Jerusalem.
    Praise the LORD!

My friend, look to Him. When you remember how great He is, your faith will soar. I promise that your seeking will be rewarded.

*Notes*

*Notes*

# 4

# IS FEAR TAUGHT?

To be honest with you, I am sitting at my desk just a little nervous about this chapter. I'm not nervous about your response. I just know that there will be very real emotions that accompany me to the places we are about to go and the people we will meet.

First, let me say that my life has been filled with an amazing and loving family. I also want you to know that I have forgiven and released those who taught me fear, but I have to talk about this. You must be aware that you are teaching those around you with everything you do every day.

I swallow back tears as I consider this chapter. A very godly lady taught me fear. She did not sit me down and say, "You need to be very afraid." No, but I watched her reactions and heard the "worry" in her prayers.

An example that I can give is the coming of the Lord, or "The rapture of the church." In her mind the coming of the Lord was a very fearful thing. "Oh, The Lord is coming back and you don't want to be left behind." Now, we need to have a healthy understanding that eternity is coming and the trumpet will sound, but I had never heard someone say how excited they were about the return of Jesus (or at least that I really noticed) until I was a married woman. It was shocking to me! What? This man was talking about the coming of Jesus and he was excited? I wanted that!

The woman also loved God with all of her heart, but did she trust His love for her? This is where faith is required. If you are living your life to please God and are saved according to His Word, you have no need to fear. He is coming for those who *love* His appearing! (2 Tim. 4:8).

She was terrified of escalators and of communicable diseases, which she warned my brother and me about at very young ages. (That one makes me laugh a little).

On the other hand, this same lady taught me so much about prayer and grace. She loved the Word of God with a fierceness. She gave me a brand-new burgundy leather Thompson Chain-reference Bible when I was around eleven years old. I read that Bible until the leather cover fell off. I still have it. She poured so much love and passion for Jesus into my heart!

What I am trying to convey is that sometimes things are so much a part of our nature (or so we think) that we don't see a need for change. It is time to search our hearts. What are we teaching those around us?

I am guilty too. I have taught my children fear, and I have repented. Now it is my mission to teach them to shut the mouth of fear in their lives. I am teaching them what faith looks like. I have heard my little girl in her bedroom saying, "Shut up, fear. You are a liar!" when she has been afraid. I am pouring into them scriptures about angels protecting them and God being in control.

*It is not too late!* Whatever you have taught your children, no matter their age, you can be an example of hope and deliverance!

Don't say, "I am just a fearful person; this is who I am." No! You are made in His Image. There is no fear in Him. As the change starts to take place in your life, you will need to remind people that you are a new person. You don't respond or react the way you did before.

> **YOU ARE MADE IN HIS IMAGE. THERE IS NO FEAR IN HIM.**

My husband and I have been married for twenty-two years. For most of those twenty-two years, my natural response was fear. Because for more than two decades my response was fear, my husband expects fear from me. I don't know how many times I have said, "Honey, I am changed! God has delivered me from fear." You know what? It's OK that I have to remind him. Every time I remind him, I remind myself.

Revelation 12:11 says, *"And they overcame him by the blood of the Lamb and by the word of their testimony."*

Remind your family, remind yourself, remind the spirit realm around you! *Therefore, if anyone is in Christ, he is a new creation; old things have passed away; behold, all things have become new" (2 Corinthians 5:17).*

As you speak these scriptures out and proclaim who you are as a new creation in Christ, you will be teaching all of those around you how to do the same! God will take whatever you bring Him, addiction, anxiety, fear, depression, and *when* He transforms you, you will be a billboard for all to see His transformative power! Your faith and the faith of those who are around you will soar!

*Notes*

*Notes*

# 5
## A DECISION TO BE MADE

Can it really be that simple? Can activating my faith really be as simple as deciding that I will trust God?

Let's see what the Word says.

"By faith Sarah herself also received strength to conceive seed, and she bore a child when she was past the age, because *she judged Him faithful who had promised* (Heb. 11:11).

How do you judge Him?

In Hebrews 11 we can read that,

> **HOW DO YOU JUDGE HIM?**

*By faith Abraham obeyed…*
*By faith Abel offered…*
*By faith Enoch pleased…*
*By faith Noah prepared…*
*By faith Isaac blessed…*
*By faith Jacob blessed and worshipped…*
*By faith Joseph gave instructions…*
*By faith Moses refused…*
*By faith the harlot Rahab believed…*

The list is so much longer still! Do you know what the common denominator is? They left everything behind, let their lives fall as they might, and put all of their confidence in God. Every person listed in Hebrews 11 had a decision to make. They judged Him *faithful*!

When fear overwhelms you to the point that you feel you cannot breathe, you have a decision to make.

Let's look at the results of the decisions made in Hebrews 11 to trust God. Hebrews 11:33–35 describes those:

> "... who through faith subdued kingdoms, worked righteousness, obtained promises, stopped the mouths of lions, quenched the violence of fire, escaped the edge of the sword, out of weakness were made strong, became valiant in battle, turned to fight the armies of the aliens. Women received their dead raised to life again. Others were tortured, not accepting deliverance, that they might obtain a better resurrection."

He is faithful!

The writer of Hebrews doesn't paint a rosy picture. He continues in verses 36–40:

> "Still others had trial of mockings and scourgings, yes, and of chains and imprisonment. They were stoned, they were sawn in two, were tempted, were slain with the sword. They wandered about in sheepskins and goatskins, being destitute, afflicted, tormented—of whom the world was not worthy. They wandered in deserts and mountains, in dens and caves of the earth. And all these, having obtained a good testimony through faith, did not receive the promise, God having provided something better for us, that they should not be made perfect apart from us."

To be honest I considered not adding these verses. I thought, "God, I'm trying to increase faith here. That's a little bit of a downer." No sooner had those thoughts passed my mind than His Spirit moved on my heart, and I saw some of you. I know that some reading this book see themselves among the second group. For those of you who are mocked, tempted, afflicted, destitute, don't be discouraged by these verses. You are known to God. He also says that this world is not worthy of you and that you will obtain a good testimony through your faith. There was purpose in what those who suffered went through. There is purpose in what you are going through. What these precious saints went through was important enough to God for it to be added to His Word. He sees you too, and He is faithful.

A precious mentor, Rev. Mike East, once said, "Trust is surrendering all control of the outcome." The truth is that we all have a measure of faith, according to Romans 12:3. When we absolutely decide that we are going to trust God, surrendering the outcome and our preconceived ideas of what the outcome should be, our faith is activated. We count Him and His knowledge and ways (that are far above ours) to be enough. We count His love for us to be eternal. We, like Sarah, count Him faithful.

Faith is not feeling, it is knowing. Knowing what? It's knowing and believing Romans 8:28.

> *And we know that all things work together for the good of those who love God, and for those who are the called, according to His purpose.*

It's believing Isaiah 55:8–9:

> *"'For My thoughts are not your thoughts, Nor are your ways My ways,' says the LORD. 'For as the heavens are higher than the earth, So are My ways higher than your ways, And My thoughts than your thoughts.'"*

(Take the time to read the verses above and below this one!)

Can someone who doesn't know Him have faith? In Hebrews 11:31 we read that Rahab was a harlot. You can read her full story in Joshua 2. Rahab did not have a relationship with God, but she was in a desperate situation and made a *decision* to trust Him. This decision of faith saved her and her household. Rahab also received what I like to call a "bonus" blessing from God. She was in the lineage of Jesus.

Matthew 1:5 tells us that Salmon begot Boaz by Rahab, Boaz begot Obed by Ruth, Obed begot Jesse. She was the great-great grandmother of King David. She had only heard of God and what He had done for His people. She knew that every enemy before the army of Israel had been defeated and that her city was next. She was a desperate woman who did not know God but made a decision to put her whole life in His hands and trust Him.

What about you? What about me? We, who have spent time in His presence. We, who have experienced His love and have basked in His presence. We do know Him, yet we doubt Him. When the answer is no. When the outlook is bleak. When the anxiety, fear, and negative thoughts try to overwhelm us, what do we do? Do we count Him faithful?

Faith over fear *is* a decision. It is a way of life. My faith *will* be stronger than the fear that is pressing down around me. It is not that fear is never present. Of course, it is. It is an emotion that comes with life, but my faith in my God is more present!

Would your name be listed in the Hall of Faith or the Hall of Fear? Is faith a testimony to your righteousness or is fear testifying on your behalf? These are not questions that you answer one time. These are questions that you answer every day and with every situation that arises. We must choose faith every day.

*Notes*

*Notes*

# 6

## FAITH WITH LEGS

For faith to be fully activated, action is required. When we put "legs" on our faith, we are reminding ourselves and those around us that faith is not just a feeling. It is a conviction that God is able. We see scriptural proof in James 2.

What *does it* profit, my brethren, if someone says he has faith but does not have works? Can faith save him? If a brother or sister is naked and destitute of daily food, and one of you says to them, "Depart in peace, be warmed and filled," but you do not give them the things which are needed for the body, what *does it* profit? Thus also faith by itself, if it does not have works, is dead.

> ... FAITH IS NOT JUST A FEELING.

But someone will say, "You have faith, and I have works." Show me your faith without your works, and I will show you my faith by my works. You believe that there is one God. You do well. Even the demons believe—and tremble! But do you want to know, O foolish man, that faith without works is dead? Was not Abraham our father justified by works when he offered Isaac his son on the altar? Do you see that faith was working together with his works, and by works faith was made perfect? And the Scripture was fulfilled which says, *"Abraham believed God, and it was accounted to him for righteousness."* And he was called the friend of God. You see then that a man is justified by works, and not by faith only.

Likewise, was not Rahab the harlot also justified by works when she received the messengers and sent *them* out another way?

*For as the body without the spirit is dead, so faith without works is dead also (James 2:14–26).*

It is very clear in scripture that works must accompany our faith. For some, like Abraham and Rahab, there is an action to be taken. For others it is believing. Sarah, for example, didn't have an "action" to give her faith "legs." She had to believe and not doubt.

> *"By faith Sarah herself also received strength to conceive seed, and she bore a child when she was past the age, because she judged Him faithful who had promised" (Heb. 11:11).*

Your mindset and the thoughts that you are dwelling on are so critical to the amount of faith you have. If you allow doubt and fear to speak to you, those will be the thoughts that rule your spirit. God was not giving us "helpful suggestions" in the Word when, in 2 Corinthians, He inspired Paul to write:

> "For though we walk in the flesh, we do not war according to the flesh. For the weapons of our warfare are not carnal but mighty in God for pulling down strongholds, casting down arguments and every high thing that exalts itself against the knowledge of God, *bringing every thought into captivity to the obedience of Christ*" (2 Cor. 10:3–5).

A very important part of our walking in faith is training our minds to bring into captivity every thought that is contrary to The Word of God. Any thought that makes you doubt Him, His Word, His love, His protection, His ability to save, or anything that The Word proclaims about Him, is *not* from Him! You have to take control of your mind.

Faith is more than just wishful thinking or thinking positive thoughts. It has to be accompanied by works, prayer, and fasting.

We see an example of this in Matthew 17.

> *And when they had come to the multitude, a man came to Him, kneeling down to Him and saying, "Lord, have mercy on my son, for he is an epileptic and suffers severely; for he often falls into the fire and often into the water. So I brought him to Your disciples, but they could not cure him."*
>
> *Then Jesus answered and said, "O faithless and perverse generation, how long shall I be with you? How long shall I bear with you? Bring him here to Me." And Jesus rebuked the demon, and it came out of him; and the child was cured from that very hour.*
>
> *Then the disciples came to Jesus privately and said, "Why could we not cast it out?"*
>
> *So Jesus said to them, "Because of your unbelief; for assuredly, I say to you, if you have faith as a mustard seed, you will say to this mountain, 'Move from here to there,' and it will move; and nothing will be impossible for you. However, this kind does not go out except by prayer and fasting" (Matt. 17:14–21).*

Sitting back "hoping" things get better or work out is not faith. Anyone can do that. You are a child of God. You know His Word. Hebrews 11:1 says, "Now faith is the substance of things hoped for, the evidence of things not seen."

What evidence do you have? I have evidence that He is faithful! This is why your testimony is so important. When I hear what God has done for you, it increases my faith that He can do the same for me. Your testimony can provide the "evidence" that someone else needs to hear. Share your testimonies of God's faithfulness.

If you have read my devotional *What Shall I Fear?* You will be familiar with the testimony that my husband and I were given a five percent chance of conceiving and now have two beautiful children. I have shared this testimony several times with my children. They know that God moved in a miraculous way to give them to their daddy and me.

A few weeks ago, we had a very desperate need in our wider family concerning a baby boy still in the womb. My niece, Taylor, had been given a very scary prognosis concerning her son Remington (Remy). We had prayed several times with our children about the need. One night as we were praying before bed my eleven-year-old son started praying for the baby again. His prayer was this: "God, the doctors said I shouldn't be here, but you brought me through. You brought me through God, and I know that you can do the same for baby Remy." He continued praying for healing over that sweet baby boy. That is faith! My son knows what God did for him when others said there was no hope, and he was *confident* that God could do the same for his baby cousin.

Dear friends, a few minutes after writing the paragraph above I got a text from my niece that she had not felt the baby move and was at the doctor's office. She called me ten minutes later to tell me that there was no heartbeat. Where is faith now?

Faith looks like my children upon hearing this news and recounting every miracle from the Bible that they could think of, telling me that God is still able to do a miracle for their baby cousin. Faith looks like my amazingly brave niece giving birth to our precious Robert Remington Stockdale, holding and loving her sweet boy. Faith looks like this young mother and father honoring his short life.

My eleven-year-old son showed me what "child-like" faith looks like while he was standing in a hospital room full of adults and wanting to remind everyone what Jesus said about a young girl in the Bible. "She is not dead, but sleeping." He reminded us all that Remington was sleeping, yes sleeping in the arms of a loving Savior. As he prayed next to me that night, I heard faith again. "God, give our family strength to get through this."

We all imagine that faith is this bigger-than-life belief that God is able, but Jesus said it can be the size of a mustard seed.

When your heart is crushed, you can still have faith. When the report isn't what you wanted, you can still have faith. How?

By trusting His Word.

> *"'For My thoughts are not your thoughts, Nor are your ways My ways,' says the LORD. 'For as the heavens are higher than the earth, So are My ways higher than your ways, And My thoughts than your thoughts'" (Isaiah 55:8–9).*

This verse brings me peace. I have put my eternity into the hands of the One who knows more, sees farther, and loves more intensely than I could ever imagine. He truly knows what is best for me and mine.

What is God asking of you? Is there a step of faith that you need to take, such as Peter walking on the water? Is it believing that he is able to do what seems impossible for you or someone you love? Is it as simple as lifting your voice and saying, "Yes! You are able! In the good, in the bad. When there are miracles and, as we read at the end of Hebrews 11, when there are not.

Your response will be your testimony! Will it be one of faith or fear?

*Notes*

*Notes*

# 7

## HOW IMPORTANT IS IT ANYWAY?

A few years ago, as I was preparing to speak at the Indiana Ladies Conference on this very topic, God kept bringing a scripture to my mind. The scripture was Revelation 21:8. In the King James Version it says,

> *"But the fearful, and unbelieving, and the abominable, and murderers, and whoremongers, and sorcerers, and idolaters, and all liars, shall have their part in the lake which burneth with fire and brimstone: which is the second death."*

To be honest, I was fighting against adding this scripture to my teaching that day. My thoughts were, "Lord, I am speaking to ladies today that are struggling with fear and anxiety. I don't want to add to that fear." I called my husband from my hotel room and told him of my struggle. He said, "Go to the verse and see what the word 'fearful' means." After hanging up, I took his advice.

**"FEARFUL" TRANLATES TO FAITHLESS.**

What I read floored me. In verse 8 of Revelation 21, the word "fearful" translates to the Greek word, "deilos; *di-los…faithless."* Strong's Hebrew and Greek Dictionary. When I saw the word "faithless," I began to weep. I understood that God was confirming His Word to me. The revelation that *to be fearful is to be faithless* overwhelmed me. As I considered all the precious saints of God that struggle with fear, something rose up in me to beat back the stronghold of fear with the Truth of God's word!

Am I condemning all those who struggle with fear? Absolutely not. I am giving a clarion call to all who struggle with fear that it is high time to trust Him. It is past time to know Whom you have believed. Daniel 11:32 says, *"but the people who know their God shall be strong, and carry out great exploits."*

You see, this really isn't about fear. It is about your relationship with Jesus. Is it important? Yes. It is eternally important. When the fear comes, for it *will* come, you have to decide whether you will let it become a part of you or whether you will choose to reject the fear and replace it with faith. It is time to be strong! How do you do this? You get into a relationship with Him. You learn His nature. You trust His Word.

Let me remind you again Who He is:

> *Now I saw heaven opened, and behold, a white horse. And He who sat on him was called Faithful and True, and in righteousness He judges and makes war. His eyes were like a flame of fire, and on His head were many crowns. He had a name written that no one knew except Himself. He was clothed with a robe dipped in blood, and His name is called The Word of God. And the armies in heaven, clothed in fine linen, white and clean, followed Him on white horses. Now out of His mouth goes a sharp sword, that with it He should strike the nations. And He Himself will rule them with a rod of iron. He Himself treads the winepress of the fierceness and wrath of Almighty God. And He has on His robe and on His thigh a name written: KING OF KINGS AND LORD OF LORDS (Rev. 19:11–16).*

This is the One who loves you. This is the One who is fighting for you. You do not have to live a life of fear. Today you can make the decision to have faith. The testimony of your life can be of one whose faith was a testimony of righteousness.

As I end this book, let's take a look at one more scripture.

> *Be anxious for nothing, but in everything by prayer and supplication, with thanksgiving, let your requests be made known to God; and the peace of God, which surpasses all understanding, will guard your hearts and minds through Christ Jesus. Finally, brethren, whatever things are true, whatever things are noble, whatever things are just, whatever things are pure, whatever things are lovely, whatever things are of good report, if there is any virtue and if there is anything praiseworthy—meditate on these things (Phil. 4:6–8).*

Do you see a plan of action here? I do. Don't worry or fret. Pray and give everything to God with thanksgiving. Tell Him what you need. This will bring you God's peace. That peace will guard your emotions and thoughts. The final verse above gives further instructions on how to *stay* in the peace that God gives you. Keep your thoughts *focused*. Keep your thoughts on what is true, noble, just, pure, lovely, a good report, virtuous, and praise worthy. You will notice that there is no room for worry or fear in this list. If you replace any fearful thought with one of these, you will maintain the peace of God in your life. You will have a testimony of faith!

Full of Fear or Full of Faith? Only you know the answer. Remember: It's not that fear is never present. It's that my faith is more present.

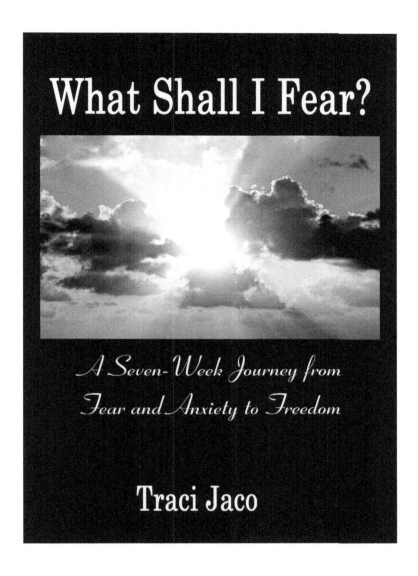

You can order Traci's first devotional

"What Shall I Fear?"

from amazon.com.

Made in the USA
Coppell, TX
11 June 2020

27384129R00046